Asina is How We Talk

A collection of Tejano poetry
written en la lengua de la gente

Praise for
Asina is How We Talk

Looking for a truly translanguaging experience con el lenguaje de la gente y con sabor del sur de tejas? Look no further: *Asina Is How We Talk* will immerse you in that wonderfully mixed and revuelto world of the tejano borderlands. Not just with the language but with the experiences y las situaciones that the poets present, we relish and bask in that borderlands ethos.

For those of us from the border living away from la frontera, away from south Texas, *Asina Is How We Talk* elicits a yearning, a deep homesickness que nos llega al corazón de lo que somos and how we talk, how we exist as Tejanos y Tejanas wishing to be en ese pedacito de tierra that we call home.

If you read *Asina is How We Talk* be ready for the richness and fullness of that translanguaging that defines us, que nos permite ser lo que somos y como somos, a true mix con elementos from both cultures, both languages, both nation states. Ambos mundos in one.

—**Norma E. Cantú**, Norine R. and T. Frank Murchison
Distinguished Professor of the Humanities, Trinity University

Asina is How We Talk, una confección--blended together by Eddie Vega-- de poetic and prosaicament expositivo verbiage escrito en el mestiza y promiscua lengua de la gentuza del Valle y far beyond, nos presenta con una multitude of rhetorical examples de uno de los más nuevos languages spoken on este watery planet de nosotros.

Nuestro down home idioma is employed by Susana Nevarez-Márquez to bring to life el ambiente de las dance halls y labor camps enlivened by la música de conjunto, by Priscilla Celina Suárez to call to mind dulces pláticas con la abuela, chats as sweet in recollection as a hot cup of café de la olla y unas empanadas o piggish marranitos, and by the inimitable Jacinto Jesús Cardona to sing-songingly rhyme into being el loquito de cada aldea mumbling resentments en la plazita y despojando a las flowers de sus pétalos.

Buy this book!

—**Arturo Mantecón**, Poet & Translator

Asina gonna write this blurbito 'cause if you're reading this book, then you're either going to understand it asina como es, or you'll think it chafo, which is not, porque esta de aquellas, and it's pura neta what the poets say here, so you might as well get yourself a caló dictionary and trucha it is 'cause el Eddie Vega and all the poets here se la rifaron. Con safos.

—**Octavio Quintanilla,** author of *If I Go Missing* and
San Antonio Poet Laureate (2018-2020)

Asina is How We Talk

A collection of Tejano poetry
written en la lengua de la gente

FLOWERSONG
PRESS

Edited by
Eddie Vega

FLOWERSONG
PRESS

FlowerSong Press
Copyright © 2022 by Eddie Vega
ISBN: 978-1-953447-87-6
Library of Congress Control Number: 2022950233

Published by FlowerSong Press
in the United States of America.
www.flowersongpress.com

Cover Image by Isabel Ann Castro
Cover Design by Priscilla Celina Suarez
Set in Candara

NOTICE: SCHOOLS AND BUSINESSES
FlowerSong Press offers copies of this book at quantity discount with bulk
purchase for educational, business, or sales promotional use. For information,
please email the Publisher at info@flowersongpress.com.

TABLE OF CONTENTS

II. LA MERA NETA

For those that taught us,
for those we will teach
y todos los demás quienes están
in between

FOREWORD

Asina is How We Talk is a fresh and tasty morsel of language activism, a defense of that nepantla of a borderland between two cultures, two languages, two nations, where even how we accent our words, which languages we speak, and whether those languages are allowed to consort with each other become a political, personal, and possibly confrontational action. An anthem of biculturalism, it fills our senses with the tastes and sounds of that cultural and linguistic mix where children of the Aztec Quinto Sol express their uniqueness and pride "...Eating pepperoni pizza/ With salsa verde..." (Nicolás Valdez) and learn that "cenizas quedan/ my body should be a furnace" (ire'ne lara silva.)

Yet still, we clamber over the obstacles with purpose and pride, despite the many attempts of traditional society to "...tempt us with the carrot/ of Spanish ancestry/ to lead us blinkered/ toward weaponized whiteness..." (David Bowles)

Often, these poems become a direct guideline for survival, instructions for living, as a person negotiating spaces between traditional choices, between the accepted cultural images, whether it's Lea Colchado's "Eat raspas with pickles and lots of chamoy..../...Keep falling in love with the moon./ Keep singing with the chicharras" ; Samantha Ceballos' *How to Stitch an Invisible Wound*; or the powerfully real multiple choice in Priscilla Celina Suarez' *HOW TO WALK AWAY*.

The incisive sarcasm of Amalia Ortiz' is a tongue-in-cheek commercial advertisement for/ warning against the escapism of mindless trend-followers in *Enough Thinkin*, in a pounding rhyme that cuts tongue right into cheek.

> Don't ask about Manteca. It all tastes better with lard.
> You'll crave it to the grave when all your arteries are hard.
> Don't ask about corn syrup. Just pass the deep fried dough.
> Don't question diabetes rates 'cause you don't want to know....

But most importantly, this collection embraces and embodies the affirmation of joyful resistance that our code-switching native Tex-Mex represents, an esthetic affirmation that regional language can be used as linguistic activism, as a documentation of our history and our oppression and our survival. Joaquin Muerte sonorously records activism "Breakin with pumas/ Danzando with plumas/ Wiping the humo from our eyes/ Fightin' the ruthless with power..."

These works also represent a decidedly dual identity and culture, a freedom of speech and of belief., the belief that no language is sanctified and prescribed by God over others, unchanging and pure, but all are mixed, and the more they mix, the richer they get, for we are all mestizos, and we are all speaking languages that have been mixed between other sources to create the "standard" languages we now speak dynamic, enriched, ever-crossbreeding and improving in their phonetic and literary wealth.

These poems shout out loud the joyfulness of being exactly who we are- half Tex, half Mex, all new, unique and fresh, like Anthony The Poet's

> ...And I don't mean to cause/
> Any controversial chispas
> With these poetic pipas,
> But I do love me
> A hand-made flour tortilla
> Filled with crispy, curly tripas!...

There are many treasures in this short volume like Rita Ortiz' *Choque en Allende, Coahuila, Mexico – 1970*, which asks questions deeper than words can pronounce. and Michelle R. Garza's confrontation of variations in bilingual individualities, *(Un)furbished History de Mi Lengua*, where

> My Spanish rolls off the tongue like
> Lego blocks—
> hard   plastic
>
> squared edges
> unwieldy at the roof of my mouth; my
> erres are covered in grease. Sluggish—
> my hot tongue tries
> to force the thick spit of my
> colonial Tex Mex away.

This is a world where
> I'm dancing all the way to the cajera
> the viejitas are smiling
> the viejitos just nod their heads
> los chamaquitos are meneando in their shopping carts, and
> my hips are swaying while I'm paying

y la cajera?
como si nada
como un stone
parada allí nomás
"veinticuatro cincuenta y tres"
it's like the music stops...
   (Eddie Vega)

and Susana Nevarez-Marquez' image-rich assertion that this is where "...
la musiquita began/ on dance floors born of earth/ packed with ceniza y
agua".

And here our world becomes populated with characters like Jacinto
Jesus Cardona's *El Bato Loco En El Zócalo*, who "scatters pétalos/ en el zócalo/
begs for pesos/ to buy besos/ for his humble/ huesos" and affirmations that
God is, after all, a Chicana who knows exactly how to build a man *bien*
'pacito, who mixes her language all the way to the end, where even love
"whispers, / ¡Te quiero singos! / y... Bueno Bye!" (Tafolla, in *God, la Chicana*.)

Gone from these pages is any shame over this interlanguage formed
by centuries of intercultural contact and the richly layered wealth of waves
of new cultural arrivals.

Asina is How we Talk is an instrument of cultural survival, pride, and
understanding, and a celebration of a dynamic translanguaging that brings
laughter, growth, and healing.

More importantly, it is a reflection of who we are, because *Asina* IS
how we talk!

—**Carmen Tafolla**
   Professor Emerita, Bicultural Bilingual
   University of Texas San Antonio
   State Poet Laureate of Texas 2015

PREFACE

Mrs. Ramirez was the toughest Spanish teacher I ever had. As a freshman at James "Nikki" Rowe High School in McAllen, TX, I had the option of taking a monolingual Spanish class (geared toward those that didn't know any or much Spanish) or the bilingual one (taught in Spanish for those that knew how to speak it but needed help with writing and grammar). My parents wouldn't have allowed me to take the easy way out in the former class, so into the latter I was enrolled. Her tongue was as heavy as her stare. There was to be no English, no mocho, no pocho, in her class. "Es 'djiste,' no 'dijites.'" "No se dice 'troka.' Es una 'camioneta.'" "Es 'así.' 'Asina' no existe." We had to drop a nickel into a jar when we said an improper word. I probably learned all that I needed to regarding "proper" Spanish in that one academic year. If not for her and her class, I probably wouldn't have been able to communicate as effectively during the year I spent in Veracruz and Oaxaca after graduating college.

She'd hate this book.

My abuelita Ofelia lived in Ciudad Mier, Tamaulipas. I spent many a summer with her and my abuelito, immersed in a language and culture different from the one in McAllen. Once, when it was becoming evident that I was having trouble rolling my Rs, she sat me down in the patio with a dictionary, having to pronounce words like "ferrocarril," and "carretera," over and over again until I said them correctly and not "como en inglés con esa erre tan floja."

She'd hate this book, too.

The colleague who scrunched her face and proclaimed, "eso no es mariachi," when I told the teacher lunch-table that I'd been to a wedding where the groom, a mariachi, serenaded his bride to Frankie Valli's "I Love You Baby," while accompanied by his fellow charro-clad musicians would probably hate this book, too. I have no doubt that many a language academic, Spanish purist, English purist, or self-proclaimed poetry lover, would hate this book.

It's not written for them.

I set out to put this book together because this is how we speak here in South Texas. I realize we're not alone in our mixing of Spanish and English, but just as the Veracruzano and the Tamaulipeco speak different Spanish and the New Yorker and the Texan speak different English, so too do the Tejano and the Nuyorican speak a different Spanglish.

We communicate in one way while in the classroom or the office, but in a total other manner when we're at home, the beauty shop, the HEB, or the taquería. Our mixed language, perhaps a hybrid or a dialect, has existed as long as people have lived in the nepantla, despite the best efforts of colonizers trying to tame wild-tongue exploits. They turn their noses up at our syntax as much as they do at our enchiladas. And worse, our children are losing the richness of this communication as our state legislature does its best to affirm one bland and homogenous cultural narrative.

I offer this collection of poetry as a celebration of the pocho, mocho, Spanglish, Tejano, Tex-Mex lengua that the gente actually speaks. Authenticity is found in being true to oneself, not in being constrained by the rules and guidelines meant to make us feel other.

In the end, I think Mrs. Ramirez and mi abuelita would each let out the big sigh of acceptance. That's all we ask of this world – give us that big sigh and accept us. Otherwise, get out of our way porque aquí estamos, no nos vamos, and asina is how we talk.

ACKNOWLEDGEMENTS

Thanks to the Luminaria Artist Foundation for their generosity in supporting this project. Special thanks go to Executive Director Yadhira Lozano for all of her effort in supporting artists and their work.

Thanks to Mateo and Diana Vega, Thiana and Frank Vera, Dominique Vega, Julián Vega, Adrienne Vann-Vega, Piper Vann-Morgan, and Jack Vann-Morgan, for all of their love and support of my work.

Thanks to Carmen Tafolla for her mentorship and contribution.

Thanks to Jacinto Jesus Cardona for his mentorship and literary advice.

Thanks to every poet that contributed work to this book.

Thanks to la raza for keeping it real and speaking como les da la gana.

I. DALE SHINE

Rita Ortiz
Words

My mother taught me words from songs her mother sang
Gave me words from her father's dichos
My mother taught me words she'd make me repeat slowly in Spanish
  Porque mija no va ser pocha!—she promised

Words that smeared gray on her fingertips
From newspaper ink telling of small happenings
Until I recognized the sound of their shapes,
I learned to memorize them, then I wanted more words
So my mother gave me books
  En Inglés también para cuando vayas a la escuela, she assured

Even though she couldn't read them en Ingles
And from puro instinto, she taught me to shape
My words on the page

David Bowles
What Do We Call Ourselves, Entonces?

Los gringos,
buenos arrieros,
tempt us with the carrot
of Spanish ancestry
to lead us blinkered
toward weaponized whiteness
like guileless subjects
of the Hispanic Monarchy.

We can't be Mexicanos
nos dicen los mexicanos
ni tampoco Mexican Americans
because we're all Americans
and to use the word
as a synonym of US citizen
is betrayal.

Forget Chicanos.
Too political. Too old school.
Too exclusionary.
Y, the eruditos remind us,
viene de los nahuas
que hablan una variety
of Nahuatl called "Mexicano,"
meshikano. Shikano. Chicano.

¿Y mestizo? Forget it, we're told.
Used by the Mexican government
to foster false nationalism
and erase Indigenous identities.
Never mind que ya vivíamos acá,
on this side of the false line,
away from that fledgling nation-state
when we started using the word.

We're de-indigenized,
people inform us,
as if we didn't know this,
as if we didn't carry the scars
of that violence on our bodies

in our souls. Cuatro palabras:
hijos de la chingada.

But when we try to rescue
something of that lost
ancestral past, when we trace
the fading threads still woven
into the fabric of our community
into the past, hoping
to re-center the Indigenous,
we're faulted for appropriating
pre-Invasion cultures
that are not ours.

Bueno, pos,
¿qué nos decimos?
In almost every Indigenous tongue,
the name for the tribe
is PEOPLE.
So what are the members
de esta nación rascuache—
¿Raza? Gente?
Watch the outsiders
narrow their eyes
and squirm in disgust.

We're like those distant ones,
the nomadic Mexihtin,
Children of Mexihtli,
who, leaving fabled Aztlan,
wandered through Chichimecah
and Huaxtecah lands
for centuries,
odiados por todos,
before founding the kingdom
of Mexihco on a little barren isle
that no one wanted
and renaming themselves
Mexihcah.

So perhaps
we are Mexihtin,
susurro quedito,
sabiendo que al rato
someone will come
to silence me.

Nicolas Valdez
Pocho'rale!

I am Pocho desde nacimiento
I eat my cheeseburger with
Jalapeños

Como Popeye y su spinach
I drink my Big Red to he finish

Empowering myself with every sip of that
Sweet red nectar

Or better yet,
I am hijo del Quinto Sol
Azteca warrior in a concrete jungle

Pues, así dice Bob Marley
"We'll forward in this generation,
Triumphantly"

There is no stereotype that can stop me
From manifesting my dreams to reality

Check your history,
I'm no mystery

You see, I was first given birth to
When Cortez first plucked that flower
From Madre Malinche's fertile womb

Pero tres generaciones han pasado
Desde'l río mis bisabuelos cruzaron

Across that dusty border land and through
The sucio Rio Grande they swam

Emerging on the other side
And now i raise my voice with pride
La gente, presente
Los Pochos para'l frente!

You see, I met this blonde
French-speaking hippie from Green Bay

She asked me to dance a merengue
Told me she was into Hip-Hop
I said, "I'm not a player I just crush alot."

Tsnaaaghhh!!

She said, "Cypress Hill's the shit!"
Had seen every Cheech & Chong flick

I said, "That's not a toothpick...."
"Oh, it is a toothpick!"

We laughed but then I realized that
This chick seemed to understand me better than
Some fresa from D.F. can

But no longer will I concern myself
With their shallow perceptions
Of this Xicano from South Texas
Because wherever I am, I am
Un Pocho, lleno de amor

Hijo del Quinto Sol
Disfrutando de la vida

Eating pepperoni pizza
With salsa verde

So, drop the chimichangas
And raise your fists
(how can you even eat that shit?)

It's time we define
These misperceptions for ourselves

So step into the water, ese
And represent

Pocho'rale!

Lea Colchado
Tejanita

Hey little Tejanita,
make sure you don't grow up too fast.
Aye, but I know how hard that can be.
Dance in the corn fields,
and climb mesquite trees.
Play jump rope with your amigas,
and chase away the boys.
Eat raspas with pickles and lots of chamoy.

Hey little Tejanita,
todo va a salir bien.
Your flour tortillas don't have to be
perfect circles.
Your hair flaps in the wind as you ride
in the back of your papá's pick-up truck.
It's apasionada,
just like you.

Hey little Tejanita,
I see you sharpening your claws,
and looking at your tíos.
No one believes you,
pero yo si.
Keep your claws so sharp,
you can gut anyone who gets too close.

Hey little Tejanita,
keep laughing underneath
those South Texas sunsets.
Keep falling in love with the moon.
Keep singing with the chicharras,
and don't grow up too soon.

Hey little Tejanita,
know that you are loved.
From your dark, long hair,

to your panzita,
all the way down to your patas.

I love you, little Tejanita,
pasa

      lo que

            pasa.

Eddie Vega
Y Empieza La Cumbia

It doesn't matter
It could be lunes o martes
Sábado o a veces en el Sunday
Pero cada vez que entro al
Culebra Meat Market

N'mbre pos,
empieza la cumbia!

Pero for real
Se abren las puertas
I walk in
y puro menea de mis hips
y mis hands go up
como asina

Because every time I'm walking in
ay 'tan Los Angeles Azules
o Los Tucanes de Tijuana
Sonora Dinamita
o pos somebody, cumbiando, you know!

But the worst
or the best, it's whatever
is when they play Fito Olivarez
y no, I don't just mean Juana la Cubana
no, the other day they were playing
        Se me sube el colesterol
        (Mi amorcito)
and I was dancing while looking for food
Se me sube el colesterol
and everything I put into my basket
was subiendo my cholesterol
(Mi amorcito)
eggs
        me sube el colesterol

and some bacon
  me sube el colesterol
pan dulcito
  me sube el colesterol
chicharrones
  que subele que subele
  que subele que subele
and I'm dancing all the way to the cajera
the viejitas are smiling
the viejitos just nod their heads
los chamaquitos are meneando in their shopping carts, and
my hips are swaying while I'm paying

y la cajera?
como si nada
como un stone
parada allí nomás
"veinticuatro cincuenta y tres"
it's like the music stops
and I wonder if maybe she prefers the corridos instead?

pero not me
porque cada vez que entro al
Culebra Meat Market on the Bandera Rd.
it's time to cumbia!

Susana Nevarez-Marquez
Conjunto Nation

La musicita began
en los sábados, los domingos
after the field work was done
la pisca de tomate, la uva, maíz,
strawberries, lettuce, oranges
toda la mesa llena

y la gente unwound
tired backs, revived
the numbness of minds
desensitized by repetition,
fatigue, ache, sun

y la musicita began
on dance floors born of earth
packed with ceniza y agua

or

if a fella could hammer and nail
and the boss didn't mind
la plataforma
apareció
como gran cuna para pies
fatigados pero alegres

porque

la musicita
revive almas,
refuerza los toques del corazón
como pasitos al ritmo
de la 'cordión
arriba y abajo
con el son del bajo sexto

la musicita humilde
de abuelos y abuelas
tias y tios
de los de la tierra
y la verdura,
todo lo básico que sostiene vida

la musicita memories of
mothers and fathers
and grandmothers and grandfathers
tias y tios,
cuentos dolorosos,
tiernos, conmovedores
lenguaje de antepasados
inolvidable

honored by memories of
children, grandchildren,
nephews, nieces,
acordionistas, guitarristas
and scholars, students,
artists, writers, poets,

y nació

Conjunto Nation

Priscilla Celina Suarez
Pan Dulce for Breakfast

an assortment of fresh outta-the-oven pan dulce
on display from El Rex in downtown McAllen.

abrazos in our greetings and short glances
at the sweet slices of heaven on the table.

Abuelita Esperanza picks out her favorite spot and
signals for the family to gather around.

the air mingles with the aroma of canela and piloncillo
from the café de olla warming on the stovetop.

clay mugs from Progresso clinking against swirling
spoons as the platica presses us into dialogues.

the morning is full of possibilities
but no plans are set in stone.

a marranito finds its way onto my plate
while the empanada de calabaza winks at me.

grandma, did you eat pan dulce as a child?
cuando nos sobraban los centavitos, m'ija.

a chocolate concha trails evidence of
where my tía travels around the room.

her mischievous laughter tells of old cuentos
and the childhoods we have all come to know.

Cesar De Leon
When You Know You Know: A Pocho Love Sonnet

you know you're la mera paipa
porque sabes parkear la troca de tu apá
bien de aquellas by the alley so no one sees us
sneak away late late you know

for a picsa and pecsi date y luego porear
& you know how to ponerle piquete
& trechas al ponche y al coo-lay if it's weak
& there better be cay-que or aque no es pore, you know?

porque lookit let me show you
how i know how
hacerle cook, hacerle clean, hacerle dust,
mapear the floors y hacerle turn on

la internet chingadera back when it goes down you know
—so we can netflix and shill

Denisse Zecca
Las Semillas de Mamá

My mamá gave me some semillas
She told me to wait and plant them hasta que estuviera al cien.
The day I plant a semilla is the day that I put everything aside to make
sure it grows bien bella y fuerte.

Mamá cargo estas semillas desde que era niña
Igual de pequeña que cuando me las dió a mi.
They were special, a legacy of womankind.

Un día decidí que era tiempo,
I would dig into mother earth and leave my mark, my precious semilla.

I wasn't alone in helping my semilla grow,
the earth was my guide y el cielo su proveedor
El cielo nos dió el sol para asegurar su felicidad
Y lluvia, to nourish her, my semilla

No me di cuenta de la decepción del cielo.
He distracted me.
Hubo un tiempo en que cayó mucha lluvia,
I put my everything into protecting my semilla from being drowned
The skies were gray for many days y la lluvia fuerte y sin remordimiento.
El sol ya no salió. El cielo gave all the sunshine away to the vecina's
garden instead.

Yet, my semilla sprouted stronger than I imagined. Resilient to the
darkness of the world.

ire'ne lara silva
donde hubo fuego

cenizas quedan
      my body should be a furnace
  all the past
      un monte entero de mesquite
         brancheslikelimbs
          and fingersliketwigs
reaching
      es que te quieren alcanzar
            tocar
            y
            quemar
cenizas quedan
      my body covered in soot grey
darklines painted
      on my face   through my eyes
         entwining circles on my
        arms breasts   belly
 long arcing lines
     racing down my thighs
             black feet
             al
             perderte
cenizas quedan
      my body's been growing rings
like trees almost
     shedding skins like snakes
     en tu ausencia
        un milagro que me conocieras
        un milagro que has vuelto
    and are my ashes warmer than
             all their
             e
             ternal fires

cenizas quedan
      my body should be a furnace

and are all our past s
            only piles of unforgiving ash
                even dust can burn
                   limbs and fingers could burn
did you know   even the
           wind won't blow away my
                     ashes
                     on
                     your skin

JR Estrada
I Wonder to Myself

I wonder to myself...what's San Antonio like to an outsider looking in...

San Antonio is your abuelita

San Antonio is your abuelita you see once a week.
And therefore, happy to see you,
The one with the bright apron and lace around the edges,
And flowers in her pockets,

She's the abuelita that doesn't understand,
What is it you do for a living,
Doesn't see how being on the
                          Computadora
Could be a job

The abuelita that you tell you've been dating your girl for nine months,
And she could tell you what other things you could've done in nine
months.

San Antonio is the abuelita with treats ready to go,
She's got paletas in the freezer,
                          Pan dulce para el cafecito,

Sweet iced-tea on the table,
Beans simmering in the pot,
                          Que crock pot ni que nada!
She's got the good flour tortillas,
Because you told her the other day
your other grandma only had corn tortillas.

She's the abuelita with the chisme,
The one with the family secret,
Who knows who has Tio's San Judas Tadeo medal,
Who saw you kiss a girl on the street,
Who knows that your mom dated your tio

Before she dated your dad
Who runs into your ex at the H-E-B,
But abuelita chats up a storm anyway
Because mijo they were so nice to me.

San Antonio is the abuelita that just loves you.

Doesn't understand what you do for a living,
Just knows that you like it,
In her old fashioned way wants you to be happy,

Doesn't care that your Spanish is not great,
That you don't eat chile,
That you're vegetarian now,
That you're not married,
That you haven't given her any grandchildren,

Doesn't care about who you're in love with today,
Yesterday and tomorrow,
San Antonio's the abuelita that doesn't care
That you were born across the river,
Born in Laredo, Houston or Austin,
Dallas, El Paso or McAllen,

                    Mira a mis niños,
                    Todos guapos,
                    Todos grandes,
                    Todos sanos,
                    Todos fuertes, lindos y contentos
The abuelita that notices that you're a bit tired,
A bit sad,
A bit thin,
Who won't make you talk about anything you don't want to,
She will, however, make you sleep and eat.

San Antonio's the abuelita
That'll adopt you,
When your abuelita's been gone a couple of years,
That'll care for you when you've been abandoned,
That takes you in when you're far from home,
Who always has a bed ready,
Even if you drop in unannounced,
Or will sleep on the floor despite

20

La diabetes,
La reuma,
La artritis,
El colesterol
La presión

The abuelita that doesn't care who you are,
What you've done,
Where you've been,

She's just glad that you're here,
In her kitchen,
Listening to her
As you allow her to take care of you,
And you're ok

"Comete un taquito, mijo."

II. La Mera Neta

Jacinto Jesus Cardona
El Bato Loco En El Zócalo

El bato loco
scatters **pétalos**
en el zócalo

begs for pesos
to buy besos
for his humble
huesos

some say
he used to be
un hombre rico

now he rocks
back and forth
chanting mil y pico
mil y pico

flashes his imaginary
machete at every fulano
zutano y mengano
who sniffs
at his delicate condition

as long as he lives
in a city
of seductive dulces
el bato loco
en el zócalo

does not have to
memorize the antidote
for poisoned arrows

Samantha Ceballos
How to Stitch an Invisible Wound

My first words—tumbled Spanish—filled my mouth with hierbabuena. Weeded out with English. I wanted to cut out my unruly tongue because it got tied too much to be tamed. When people mispronounce your surname enough, you begin to question from where you came, that valley between cultures donde nunca eres suficiente. Where balanced identities are a myth you dig for. My parents delicately cut us from the wound placed us in water, and buried us anew, but, sometimes, transplantations do not take. Roots remember la tierra madre that helped germinate them. My tongue still flowers with ancient words rooted deep in my taste buds. Though twice removed, I rip open the scar with every question, pack the dirt tight, and hope new vines will stitch me shut.

Mia Stahl
Mountain Laurel

My mother dreamed of a life free of the brokenness that built her,
                                            She ached for
                                    Monochrome
                                            Simplicity
                                                    Quiet

A life wiped clean of the color that stained her soul.

The color of sweet sandía juice, dripping on the Saltillo floor that would later
make her nauseous every time she thought of her father.

Her mother's hand built like hammers,

Every problem she ever encountered a nail.

Los angeles reminded mi abuelita that a second chance could come in a bottle
of cotton and light. All the while her girls, built of stone and mortar, rest on her
back. She would kiss the cheek of God every Sunday and never truly know peace.

Pepa's lungs, built of Juarez iron, would breathe life into thirteen God-fearing
bodies,

One would lose his hand,
        Another his young life,
        Two their sight,
        Three their freedom,
        Four their memories,
        Another her child,
        And the last her compassion.

She would be the one who stayed to powder her mother's breasts, to wash her
hair, to make her conchitas.

My hands built like mountain laurel petals, would start working at the age of
sixteen, not of need, but by choice.

My heart made of Juarez iron, built to withstand the aftermath of a family of
women shot down by the very world they wished to build up.

My brain a hammer, every injustice a nail.

My soul stained with the color of my mother's blood, the color she has worked
tirelessly to erase.

Cesar L. de Leon
new rules for grieving boys

don't let the knots in your throat become
heads to bury in pillows of mud

don't anchor el vacío in your pecho
al hambre y la sed

solloza y tiembla
in fear and memory

free the tides under your rib cage
allow yourself to be a moon

unshackle your silhouette
form the armature of muscle and bone

for other men to admire
touch

ire'ne lara silva
tierra

there are days when   i   wake
with the taste of   tierra in my mouth
                         i
            eat and taste tierra
            speak and taste tierra
it has gone deep in me
            i can smell it on my skin   like the earth
before rain   i
               taste salt and green things on the
tip   of my tongue   in every word
everything   i   eat has the edge
            of earth in my mouth   a grittiness of sand
against my teeth   i
                         feel caracoles and roots
crystals and leaves
                         blood on my tongue
               i
                         taste tierra when
i look at the sky
               when   i take a step the earth
swallows me   i have swallowed it
i taste it   it tastes me every time
                         i   breathe it in
esta tierra es tuya   yo soy de la tierra
maíz tastes like tierra   y sal y sudor and my blood in

my veins tastes like tierra
               to my flesh your mouth tastes
like tierra   i
drown in zoquete   grow roots into your flesh
               i
                         swallow salt from your skin
            know you are part of the earth part of me
but not mine   i am not yours
               we belong to the tierra
            esta tierra es mía yo soy de la tierra

30

tierra

that birthed me
darkened me   fed me
            cradles me still

Priscilla Celina Suarez
How to Walk Away

1. Figure out your lenguaje.
    a. You are a Tejana, but that does not give you
        the right to forget your lisp.
    b. Eres de la frontera, but you must mask your
        desire to run once you belong.
    c. You'll never fit in anywhere.

2. This is extremely important.
    Stop being a preguntona because:
    a. Your tía-abuela will think you are metiche.
    b. Nobody really cares about the connections
        you try to find through your family tree.

3. Remember how you loved clubbing en La Zona Dorada?
    a. Forget it ever existed because those are secrets
        between you, your primos, and the borrachera days.
    b. It's not like La Zona remembers your name.

4. Nescafe is meant to be shared during merienda.
    a. You don't have time to merendiar anymore.
    b. Nescafe will cut ties with you because of Starbucks.

5. Are you a U.S. Citizen as you cross borders?
    a. Yes or no?
    b. If yes, why are you afraid of the migra?
    c. It's a simple question.
    d. Are you sure you belong?

Amalia Ortiz
Enough Thinkin'

Enough thinkin' time for drinkin'!
Bust out a cascarón y quiebralo!
Enough thinkin' time for drinkin'!
Let's toast Fiesta San Antonio!

Enough thinkin', time for drinkin'
Don't ask me why we party. I don't know.
We owe less thinkin' and more drinkin'
Thanks to the Order of the Alamo!

Don't learn the history behind the party in the streets
Don't question why el pueblo celebrates its own defeat
Don't question how Católicos converted Indios
No piense en quien perdió ni en que perdieron o quién ganó.

Los Indios, Los Indios called this land Yanaguana
Before the priest renamed it San Antonio de Padua
Los Indios were beaten until they spoke their Spanish right
Then the Czech and German settlers ran them off 'cause they weren't white

Forget the Texians who stole Téjas de México.
No piensen en quien perdió ni en que perdieron o quien gano.
Don't question social constructs of the rich Southern elite.
Don't ask. Let's just get shitfaced and buy something else to eat.

Enough thinkin' time for drinkin'!
Compra un funnel cake y cómelo!
Enough thinkin' time for drinkin'!
Let's toast Fiesta San Antonio!

Don't ask about Manteca. It all tastes better with lard.
You'll crave it to the grave when all your arteries are hard.
Don't ask about corn syrup. Just pass the deep fried dough.
Don't question diabetes rates 'cause you don't want to know.

Don't pass me any veggies. Just serve me extra meat.
I'll wash down my blood pressure meds with beer after I eat.
I'll get the midnight munchies, and eat more after that
Flautas, gorditas, puffy tacos – no wonder we're fat!

No pensamos que comemos ni en aumentar de peso.
No piense en dieta sólo cúbrelo con queso.
And spread on extra mayo to my corn in a cup
It's not fiesta until I see somebody throw up

Enough thinkin' time for drinkin'!
Oíga! El Chicken Dance!   Pues Báilalo!
Enough thinkin' time for drinkin'!
Let's toast Fiesta San Antonio!

Enough thinkin', time for drinkin'
Don't ask me why we party. I don't know.
We owe less thinkin' and more drinkin'

Rita Ortiz
Choque en Allende, Coahuila, Mexico - 1970

The headline on the *Zócalo* from Piedras Negras, Coahuila
In December 1970 read
      Fue a visitar a su novia y por poco muere!

My father watched them burn after the bus crashed
Veníamos de Allende. Fui a visitar a tu madre
Semanas antes de la boda, he recounted with a slight smile
Setting down his mug

Fue en un Diciembre antes de Navidad, he muttered
Then cleared his throat, *Cuando chocó el camion.*
Somos pocos los que sobrevivieron.
I could imagine the dry, cold air, flames on sandy earth
Desperate pleas replaying his memory in my mind

He can still hear them burn, *Una señora, gritaba por auxilio*
The woman he said he couldn't save fills
A small bubble in my morning coffee with her screaming
I can picture my father lying on the ground with burns
A fresh wound on his face—the scar in his wedding photo

Living or dead, we all keep burning don't we?
I thought, but did not say it.
He poured me a second cup.

Odilia Galvan Rodriguez
At the Aquí Me Quedo

He lived most days
at the Aqui Me Quedo
A cantina
between Harlingen
and Lyford
Se quedaba allí diokis

No'mbre his familia
didn't know
thought he was at the jale driving
the cotton picking maquina
pero no, he lost it
llegaba bien pedo
fell off the driver's seat
one too many times

Te distes cuenta
cuando huistes a las vistas
esa vez con tu amigo Jose
he said, my dad sees your jefito
down at the cantina a lot
como tu le caivas mal a los padres del
you thought, it must just be chisme
your dad was at work
so you left it at that

Entonces one day
you told your 'Ama
what Jose had said
because your dad
was coming home
drunker and later
than usual

but she said
no'mbre
no puede ser
no seas chismosa
mondada
o te dare
con el chicote
en las nachas
a todos modos
'amonos pa' ya

y hacina fue
como encontramos
'Apa todo borracho
acostado
sobre la barra
a las doce de la tarde
allí en el *Aquí Me Quedo*

III. ÓRALE

Carmen Tafolla
Don't let them treat you like toast...

(Para los jovenes de todas edades,
los que estan luchando, tratando, dudando, continuando.)

Don't let them treat you like toast
when you're really pan dulce,
Sweet bread   rising high   blooming to the fire
Steaming fresh   and hot   out of the oven.
No, you are NOT Cool.
You are Just. Plain. Hot.
Hot like chile fresco, like salsa picante
Hot like tamales, hot like home!
Hot spirit, hot style, hot-hearted
Caliente hot, and hot a lot.

And if they mock you, say you're not cool,
while they sit cold, making up the rules,
Those chifladitos ain't worth a bag
of nuestros Flaming Hot Cheetos.

You are flowing like the liquid lava
of lover volcanoes, El Popo & Ixta,
filled with passion, filled with heat.
So let your voice erupt
with the healing energy of smoke,
besos desde el deepest core...
to Say – No, Señor! No, Señorita!
Say – Seño', SIR! I make my rules,
And rule my words, and know
My worth.
Say - Wátchate! Caution!
I own a molcajete
And I know rete-bien
how to use it.
Say - Cuida'o   cause right now
Straight out of this steamy orno
I am rising hot and ready

Wátchate! While we cook up
something full of flavor,
full of our souls' calor,
full of me, the way I am.
Say, Yo soy
Pan dulce- sweet bread of life,
<u>hot</u>   out of the oven.

Daniel Garcia Ordaz
My Carnalito Is A Real Tragoncito

Después de nine months un milagro ocurrió.
My little brother was born—
y comió y creció.

Our 'Amá gave him pecho—
pero, in fact, de hecho,
no era enough.

So, le dieron formula—
y se puso bien buff.

Desde que he was chiquito—
he's been bien panzoncito.

Everyone dice
que está bien sanito.

Now que he's able, se sienta en la table—
y nunca deja de comer.

La semana pasada
he ate carne deshebrada—
shredded beef tacos (too many to count)!

Antier se tragó un pastel de chocolate—
pero todavía he wanted merienda.

Ayer se atarantó two paletas de coco—
but that foo todavía was bien tragoncito!

Hoy desayunó three eggs over-easy—
con pancakes al lado, y ham.

Mañana who knows what he'll wake up to eat—
¡Tal vez four burritos or maybe pig's feet!

Pero now su pediatrician
Es bien trucha con nutrition—
y está bien concerned—
so, she gave him a dieta—

"Just to see how it goes."

Mom's kinda sad porque
she loves sus chubby forearms
sus chubby little toes.

On Mondays para comenzar—
ensalada de frutas para el paladar.

On Tuesdays para su alimentación—
flown in from Japan ¡Un caldo de tiburón!
(Well, that's what we tell him,
pero it's just camarón!)

On Wednesdays para rellenar—
se lo van a llevar
to a vegetarian sushi bar.

On Thursdays para merendar:
lonches de lechuga—
instead of white bread—
while visions of pan dulce
dance in his head.

On Friday—it's pizza night—
but for him pa' cenar—
A bunless hamburger
para no engordar.

On Saturday—Dios mío—
nomás le van a dar
vegan hot dogs con fake mayonesa—
so he can rebajar.

Los Domingos he's free to eat as he pleases—
Quesadillas and nachos with all kinds of cheeses.
Pero, like Cinderella, the party can't go too late.
Whatever he eats must be eaten by eight.

Once he gets healthy
Ya no tiene que stress.
I know this hurts,
Pero la doctora knows best.

Dicen que los babies flaquitos
no son tan cute como los gorditos.
Pero no es easy tener healthy looks
Cuando our madrecitas are such bad ass cooks.

Y también our abuelitas
Are siempre listesitas
To share their galletitas
¡Con un tecito or café calientito!

No le hace que my carnalito
For right now está gordito.

Al rato with a little more time
Mi little bro va a estar lookin' fine.

¡So, keep your chin up, Carnal!
¡No te rajes! ¡Dale shine!

Joaquin Muerte
We Ometeotl

We Ometeotl
Hablando Macehual within a séance
Breakin with pumas
Danzando with plumas
Wiping the humo from our eyes
Fightin' the ruthless with power
who despise
our culture infusing reinforcement foundation influence
introducin' the true fortune of music
from its distorted illusion
seducin' with hip hop acoustic fusion
inducin' euphoric states
conduce to make your neck loose
no one diminishes fakes like
this Mexica star gazer the cosmic ranger
you've engaged in unexplainable outrageous amounts of misplacement
and abusive
I gain hatred
The tone is tasteless
I mean no flava
Its bland
I need to gain strength
Allow the universe to expand my DNA strand
I seek to gain land
Once stolen
Tabacco and sage rollin'
Mind, body and soul emotion is the alter
I pray with sacrificial flesh when I falter
Behold the conscious mind an evolutional time
will come
As I make lyrics succumb
To beats with heat
Hotter than the earths core

Styles influence volcanoes, storms and monster of folklore
Thoughts to make your soul soar
Across the heights amongst the heavens
With essence of incandescent fluorescent luz
Concentrate and abstruse
Demanding Knowledge, wisdom and overstandin'

Prayer
Face East, West, North South
We ask permission to let us live
And bless the path of our heritage

Face East, West, North, South
Tlazlokamati Ollin in Nahui
Mexica Tiahui

Face East (EL!)
West (EL!)
North (EL!)
South (EL!)

Anthony The Poet
TACO CITY U.S.A.

As long as it's tender,
Pero not too aguada,
I will probably order the tacos
De carne guisada.

There are days
When I will pray upon my hands and knees
For bean and cheese,
And even weep as I beg
For dos de bacon and egg.

When I was a kid,
All my dad would ever get us
Was papas con huevo,
Until we finally protested—

"Por favor, papá... queremos algo nuevo!"

Sometimes,
It's los chiquitos
De las taco trucks que yo canto,
Looking so holy
They seem like they were dropped from
The Virgen de Guadalupe's santo manto,
Sprinkled on top with cebolla,
Limón, y un poquito de cilantro!
And I still get confused

When they make me choose
Between al pastor and carne asada;
Les quiero decir,
"Give me BOTH, o no me den nada!"

Es muy sencillo—
I'll do picadillo if I have to;

It's fine—
But unlike my tío,
I don't want any little pieces of potato
In mine!

In honor of my grandmother's favorite,
Y por todo lo que hizo,
Sometimes I will order
Tacos de frijolitos con chorizo!

A veces,
What I most want
Is to find
A little hole-in-the-wall restaurant
With tacos de chicharrones con chile
Tan picosos,
Que te hacen llorar y sudar,
Even though they're so deliciosos!

Once a year,
My vegetarian friends,
Who, instead of meat,
Would rather eat
Flowers and tree bark
And even zacate,
Convince me to try a taco
Made with fresh tomate con aguacate.
Oh, you should hear
Their sudden gritos,
When I introduce them
To taquitos de nopalitos!

And I don't mean to cause
Any controversial chispas
With these poetic pipas,
But I do love me
A hand-made flour tortilla
Filled with crispy, curly tripas!

I did not know this as a child,
But I surely know it now—

They are definitely the smelly,
But super-tasty entrails of a cow!!!

For truly special occasions,
Just like Mick Jaeger,
I have a feathery, pink boa
That I use to wipe my cheeks
As the grease drips down my face
When I bite into my favoritos
Tacos de barbacoa!

There's nothing
That really rhymes with "lengua,"
But I have no problem in saying
As this story is sung—

I will walk into any congalito
On Nogalitos
And say,
"Come on, people,
Just give me some tongue!!!"

This is Taco City U.S.A., Güey!
And you'll find good ones
In every directional way!

Tacos, tacos,
All kinds of tacos—
The list never ends:

But the best tacos of all
Are the ones that we share
With familia and friends!!!

Tiffany Galvan
Somos Mujeres

Blessed are you, Mujer

With your skin, the color of the clay from which you were formed so
        perfectly
The seed that gave birth to your hopes, fears, and dreams

To the mujeres that carried the world within them
To the mujeres, that carried the world on their shoulders
As they toiled the fields, searching for hope among the flowers
Searching within the dying embers of their hearts,
But never ceasing to come up with ways to show their sazón

From the crook of the smile they hid behind
To the sway of the hips that helped them carry the load
To the hands that formed the maza
That filled the bellies of our future
Wrapped in the abrazos of only a mother's love

The hands that rubbed the healing eggs to rid us ninxs from ojo
And the legs that carried them on their walks to freedom

For the stories that they told of resiliency
Through the tears and bloodshed that is native to this Earth,
Our spirits soared like the eagles they pretended we weren't

The snake that foretold our land, but sold us out with the apple of the
        Spaniard's eye

In full bloom the dandelion shines like the sun,
And with a gust of wind, the dandelion seeds multiply like flowers that
still bloom through concrete

They tried to erase our history,
But they didn't know that our native spirits have risen—
For we are the children's children of a dying mother's wish.

Tomás Roque
Familia

The soundtrack to my earliest memories is composed by
David Lee Garza and Jay Perez
De niño I would fall asleep to sound of thirty or more people,
who would be laughing and dancing to Tejano lullabies
a couple of hours
before they became wolves
      howling gritos at the moon.
 a long night sprinkled with a montón or so
of noise complaints from the vecinos
       was the only way my family saw fit to send off any loved one

To this day,
should diosito decide to call another one of our pack home,
you can find the rest of us,
huddled around a barbecue pit,
wrapped in a backyard of memories or possibilities,
      depending on your age
near a radio blaring heart aches or headaches,
      depending on your age

If there's anything my family knows how to do,
      other than drink,
it's come together.
a tradition of outstretched arms has built us stronger than levees,
taught us that rains may come and go,
but as long as la luna still shines flood lights bright enough to dance to,
then there's something worth celebrating

My familia loves to remind each other that
someone, alguien
will always be on the other end of the receiver,
that there is an ocean of couches to surf.
that our legacy is more than just
cloudy memories and life lessons some of us were
too young to watch play out,

that these family reunion scriptures will be preached
　　　to breathe faith into the generations we give birth to,
psalms to teach us that even though we watch over each other
　　　more diligently than angels,
there are still ghostS and skeletons in our midst that prove
　　　we are only human,
y en esos dias when wilting feels like the only way to grow,
there is divinity in having your spine held up by people who just might
love you more than the heavenly Father himself,
and no matter how wayward our path may take us,
family hands will always be bound with hopes and well-wishes,

I believe diosito could find himself in the forgiveness
passed down through generations,
and even if he doesn't,
I can't think of a better place to start looking

Carmen Tafolla
God, La Chicana

God sure knew what She was doin
when she made You, mi PapiChulo.
She knew how to put that big montonote of risa and readiness
right at the core, before even inserting the corazón!

Wrapped it in ternura and courage,
acomodándolo entre those lungs singing out your song of life
sin miedo, and those guts, always ready for adventure.
She put it entre esa voz de mariachi, velvet y romántico,
y un estómago bien loco, hungry always for el sabor
de la vida.

La God, she wrapped it all en un paquete bien perty,
un alma puro party, y una sonrisa twenty-four seven,
infinitely generoso, and 360 degrees wide.

Echale un bigote,   a treasure chest of alegría y amor,
la voluntad to luchar against injusticia,
and ojos bailando con respeto para toda criatura,
saludando al janitor, a la 4-year-old, y al college president
con el mismo entusiasmo y honor...

y Milagro of all Miracles,
amándome a mí
sin condición
y sin fronteras.
amándome a mí
until you took my breath away.

God, la Chicana,
la que habla Tex-Mex,
She sure knew what She was doin
when She made You, mi Chulo,
from the momento exacto in which you cumbia'd into this world
to the very last moment in which your eyes smile

an infinity of amor and whisper,
¡Te quiero singos!
y ...
Bueno, Bye.

IV. Dale Gas

Darian Danielle Rodriguez
Pocha

How does my Spanish offend you?
"You're just not that Mexican!"
My Spanish isn't a full-grown woman
she is still growing
I let her loose when I bang my pata on the sofa,
a quick
AYE CHINGOW!
and once again I am being told I am a "coconut"

How does my Spanish offend you?
My Spanish knows how to dance every cumbia
and grew up listening to
Ramon Ayala, La Mafia and Emilio Navaira
on early Saturday mornings as my mother cleaned our casita
from top to bottom with Fabuloso

My Spanish knows the purple Fabuloso is the ONLY Fabuloso

My Spanish is Chicano Spanish
It's the kind of Spanish that translates gringo slang like
"Go get em' tiger!" into "Dale Shine!" and
"Hey what's up dude?" into "que pasa guey?"

My Spanish comes from cholos and cholitas
who turned lowrider engines into altares
and taught us to pray to the power that lives only in our hands
power my abuelos picked from the tierra as migrant workers
working for a better life across Los Estados Unidos

So again I ask, how does my Spanish offend you?
how is my Spanish less than yours?
hasn't our gente suffered through nough borders?
why are you erecting walls around my tongue?

My Spanish isn't a full-grown woman,
she is still growing
I let her loose to laugh con mi Abuela in a language her mind feels free in
I let her loose last week as I fought for the 15-year-old Honduran refugee
who had been sleeping outside but still coming to my classroom every
day to learn

So por favor, no mas dime how my Spanish isn't enough for you?
"Well it's because we're from the Valley!!"
Oye, let me tell you something, your proximity to Mexico
does not provide you with a seal of approval
and a welcome basket full of tamales, pan de polvo and a six-pack of
Modelo okay,
you are right though, I'm not from the valley

I'm from the land of palm tree dreams,
a holy place where La Reina de Tejano watches over her gente
Selena's Spanish wasn't full grown either and her father summed it up
like this:
"Mexican-Americans have to be more Mexican than the Mexicans and
more American than the Americans, it's exhausting!"

So go ahead and call me a "coconut"
or a pocha
or whatever the fuck makes you feel like a "real Mexican"
I'll laugh it off with a "no mames guey"
on an early Saturday morning as I clean my own casita
con purple Fabuloso
and when I bidi bidi bom bom a little too hard and hit my pata en la sofa
otra vez
I promise you the first words out of my mouth will still be
AYE CHINGOW!

Jacinto Jesus Cardona
TEX-MEX CODE-SWITCHING

Code-switching my Tex-Mex linguistic twitch Spanish English leap into
my speech bewitching code-switching shifting from one linguistic code
to another can cast a spell on you no it's not a hex to flabbergast to
stupefy to vex monolingual speakers code-switching just my joy of dos
dos idiomas two languages in a conversation an alternating current a
high-power application Luigi Luigi Galvani experimenting with electricity
took a copper hook frog legs twitch the rest is galvanizing history just
like el dos dos de febrero when the 1848 Treaty of Guadalupe Hidalgo
ended the war between the U. S. and Mexico and Mexicans who
stay in Texas become Mexican-Americans caught between speaking
Spanish and speaking English making the most of a linguistic hop la raza
cósmica become grammatical grasshoppers chapulines creating a code-
switching chapulínguistics we got hops nonetheless at school a child
gets a spanking for speaking Spanish goes home to trace a favorite font
blackletter aka Old English or Gothic some say just speak all in English
or all in Spanish but when my mother dropped her purse she exclaimed
Ay chihuahua se me calló la purse so I say love that you know the word
purse love that you know bolsa yes my mom should have said Ay se me
calló la bolsa but she did not and I like to think she was celebrating the
hybrid hyphen in Mexican-American the hybrid hyphen in code-switching
hybrid is now cool hybrid cars hybrid learning hybrid ink pens and hey hey
witness a code-switching NBA Los Spurs Los Lakers Los Nuggets before
hybrid was main-stream I remember my students at John F. Kennedy High
School Los Rockets in San Antonio telling me sir guess what los Spurs
won last night sir los Spurs because los is so cool los los dos dos Ay Dios
mío se me calló la purse cool code-switching bewitching chapulínguistics

Armando X. Lopez
Shursheees!

My job is to frustrate you pinche Castillians and Victorians.
I pronounce words with unfettered joy and absolutely no shame,
making you cringe on the inside
while you smile sheepishly on the outside,
as I order shurshee's fried shicken with sheese on my fries!

Watcha, look at the way that I navigate through the King's Englich
While I mess up el spanich de la reyna de españa....All to your CHAgrin!
Asking you for a chit of paper,
to write down my mocho pocho language.
Don't try to shaange me,
I am here to stay... and I've been here for a long time.
You wish that you could hide me.
But nimodo... you can't
Porque the rain in Spain falls mainly in the plain
Pero it's chispiando over by the walemar!
Right here on the border where languages and cultures
crash into each other
like a marble cake, all swirly in the middle
You want a place with no boundaries... try the words
that come out of my mouth.

This is the true frontier! This is where the function of language is
To communicate, not by rigid grammatical patterns
that stick to one tongue.
But falling all over itself, in the true tower of babel where
many linguistic versions (not that kind of virgin) are vomited
onto the landscape.
Basketball is balon sesto, snarls the purist!
Not here profe. It's basquetbol!
And in most conversations in Laredo's heat
you can't get through one sentence without a little mix:
Like, "*I went to the mall pero no haye parking so me fui!*"
And the best part es que te entendi!

So get over it! If you want for it to be pure,
go back across the Atlantic where
Spain and England have many dialects of their own languages .
There's no place that doesn't bend the language one way or another.
For as they say, with a wink… en nalgotras partes de Tejas
I am fixing to go..y
No se dice porfis, se dice pretty please…

And while in Roma, pues, osea, majority rules.
And some will speak mostly English…
And others will speak only Spanish,
But how do you say iPad in Spanish, or horchata in English.
And when the music plays there's no word like chanclear.
No drink like a coke of orange,
No song like the star-spangled banner that begins with that
All-American lyric, Jose, can you see!

So don't stress out when I need to get the Ch sound right I can say it.
And I say it Like this: No Chingues!

Pepe García Gilling
No Accent-o

you don't even have an accent, compliment. *fucking mexican*, insult. flip
and flop, speak American cause i can't won't speak mexican. I can. I speak
Mexican. Norteño. Costeño. Defeño. Sureño. Valluco. Pachuco. Tacuache
cuh. look for the yellow letters at the bottom of my screen were/are the
best english teacher i ever had. VHS hit play and repeat. trailer park home
dad's back from school to teach me to ride a bike. mamá me pone la tina,
cause ant bites left and right. memories of a girl that came from the forest.
papá called her "la caraja", i think she was white I think she was cool. bus
ridin' and mexsplaining that it's called fútbol, not soccer. kids laugh. I score
easy while coach sheriff tells my mom about the gangas. mamá wants to
know where the sale is. coach sheriff says gangas are gangs not sales. *Pepito
sigue hablando inglés*, dicen mis primos, primas. switchin' my code back
to Costeño. Tampiqueño. Uruguayan neighbors ask my tía for her chichis
(toys). *ay, sebastián, son juguetes.* mamá english teacher in Monterrey. She
lived in the states. forgot to mention hacedora de vestidos in her resumé.
we're told to wipe our mouths with shakespeare in high school, we never
once talk about Cortázar or Sor Juana. One classroom down, el profe
that lets us eat in class, a vato wanted for tax evasion in the states. Mug
shot in the papers. i practice my inglés with european students. i say *y'all*
and produce a southern gringa friend. years later she goes to costa rica,
where maes say teja y chante and tattoo pura vida under their skin while
listening to Marley. i can (sorta) do an irish accent, so i do entire spiels
about plastic snakes in kingdoms with the rodent king, same mouse who
created a genie who taught me slang, an elephant that showed me it was
okay to have acid trips, a Native American sing to white-colored winds that
welcome Conquistas. VHS hit play and repeat. hit play and repeat. hit play
and repeat. hit play and repeat. the words come in english, they do. they
sound scratchy. luego, they say i can write in Spanish. so I do. fluyen. se
escurren de mi boca a mi pluma. my words are mis historias. I am bilingüe.
sin acento. dicen. when I get there I see the brown and black bodies, drifted
from South to north. across wired fences and language borders. tired feet.
tired hands. their angelito comes up to me. she asks me for my story. so
she listens and, god bless her, she says

you don't even have an accent, compliment.

this time I'm okay with it.

Michelle R. Garza
(Un)furbished History de Mi Lengua

My Spanish rolls off the tongue like
Lego blocks—
hard   plastic

    squared edges
unwieldy at the roof of my mouth; my
erres are covered in grease. Sluggish—
my hot tongue tries
to force the thick spit of my
colonial Tex Mex away.

Amá dice que
Spanish is important—businesses
look for bilingual employees,

but her school beat her
lengua out of her
head—tried to replace it
with ~~wild American spirits~~—

Cowboys
Texas rangers
and now

they want to build
Skyscrapers in my mouth—land
their jets between the ridges of my palate
sacrifice my smile to the
Tech gods in zoom
and in fotos.

My lengua is a puzzle,
symbols in their pamphlets, broken
apart and pulled together
in clean   straight lines

They dig for gold inside my throat.

The neighborhood borracho   still
reeks of Bud Light

I want to find words to tell him
You deserved better.

My tongue fights

hard to remember how

pero no me recuerdo

                      de nadie

CONTRIBUTORS

David Bowles is a Mexican American author and translator from south Texas. Among his many award-winning titles are *Feathered Serpent*; *Dark Heart of Sky: Myths of Mexico*; *The Smoking Mirror*; and *They Call Me Güero*. His work has been published in multiple anthologies, plus venues such as *The New York Times*, *Strange Horizons*, *Apex Magazine*, *The Dark*, *Latin American Literature Today*, *School Library Journal*, *Rattle*, *Translation Review*, and the *Journal of Children's Literature*. Additionally, David has worked on several TV/film projects, including *Victor and Valentino* (Cartoon Network), the *Moctezuma & Cortés* miniseries (Amazon/Amblin) and *Monsters and Mysteries in America* (Discovery). Learn more at www.davidbowles.us and follow him on Twitter @DavidOBowles

Jacinto Cardona is a San Antonio, Texas, poet who grew up in Alice, the Hub of South Texas. He is the author of *Pan Dulce*, a poetry book. His poem "Bato Con Khakis" was selected for performance at the New York City Symphony Space. He is a *La Voz de San Antonio* Poetry Champion and his poetry is documented in *Voices from Texas* by San Antonio filmmaker Ray Santiesteban. Cardona teaches English at Incarnate Word High School.

Samantha Ceballos is a Chicana poet and scholar. She is a proud Tejana who was born in Brownsville but grew up in Katy and currently lives in San Antonio. The Borderlands have always been a central topic in her creative and scholarly writings. Her works have appeared in various publications including *El Mundo Zurdo 7* and the *Boundless 2020 Anthology*. Samantha will graduate with her MA in Literature, Creative Writing, and Social Justice from Our Lady of the Lake University in May 2021 and will be attending the University of Texas for a PhD in English.

Lea Colchado is a native of Harlingen, Texas and spent her childhood playing in the corn fields and singing with the chicharras under the warm Valley sky. She currently lives in San Antonio where she teaches English at Our Lady of The Lake University, and is passionate about language and stories, especially from Tejanas (and Tejanitas) of the Valley.

César L. de León is one of four poet-organizers for Poets Against Walls, a grass-roots collective of poets and educators dedicated to centering and elevating work by Borderland writers, artists, and activists affected by borders and divisions of all kinds. Other projects he has worked on include workshops and fundraisers with other writers and activists benefiting local communities in the Rio Grande Valley of Texas and elsewhere. His work has appeared in *Queen Mob's Tea House*, *Pilgrimage*, *The Acentos Review*, *La Bloga*, and the anthologies *Pulse/Pulso: In Remembrance of Orlando*, *Imaniman: Poets Writing in the Anzaldúan Borderlands*, and *Dreaming: A Tribute to Selena Quintanilla-Perez* among others. Cesar's first collection of poems, *Speaking with Grackles by Soapberry Trees* is forthcoming from FlowerSong press in 2021.

J.R. Estrada is a writer and poet from El Paso, TX living and teaching in San Antonio. His work has been featured in the San Antonio Express-News, the Houston Chronicle, and El Paso Community College's Chrysalis Literary Journal.

Anthony "The Poet" Flores is a 3-time San Antonio Grand Slam Poetry Champion who has represented the city in competition on six different occasions at the National Poetry Slam. He has performed his work all over the United States, from local schools and community centers to HBO's Def Poetry Jam to the Lincoln Center in New York City. He is a co-founder of Fresh Ink Under-21 Youth Poetry Slam, and has worked with over 20,000 kids and teens over the past decade. A few years ago, he founded The University of The Spoken-Word, a collective of spoken-word artists that has performed at some of the city's most high-profile cultural events. His widely popular "Manu Ginobili" poem was published in 2018 as part of the Manu Ginobili Tribute Poster by the San Antonio Express-News, and he was named "Best Local Poet" in the San Antonio Current's "Best of San Antonio 2018" issue. He released his first full-length book of poetry, *CINCUENTA*, in January of 2020. He is a full-time poet who lives and works on the Southside of San Antonio.

Tiffany Galvan is a San Antonio native. She is the founder/CEO of TMG Media, LLC, a firm that empowers BIPOC non-profit leaders with proven strategies to effectively share their stories, missions, and raise money for their communities. Since 2020, she has served over 170 clients, and helped them raise millions of dollars across the US, Canada, Africa, and the Philippines. Tiffany's writing and work is reflective of her experiences with grief, mental health, trauma, resilience, community, community-building, ancestors, and the non-profits field.

Pepe García Gilling is a writer, filmmaker and teacher originally from Tampico, Tamaulipas, México. He's currently completing his MA in Spanish after finishing his MAIS in Mexican American Studies and his MFA in Creative Writing, all at UT Rio Grande Valley. He has three independent short films that have been screened at several film festivals around the world and two have been picked up for distribution and are streaming on Amazon Prime and Vimeo Plus. Recently, his feature screenplay "Border Flesh" won the Platinum Remi Award in the Horror/Thriller category at the 54th WorldFest Houston International Film Festival. Most of his films, his writing, and his academic work focus on issues of Latinx representation and the particular experiences of border life and culture.

TEDx Speaker **Daniel García Ordaz**, a.k.a. The Poet Mariachi, is the author of *Cenzontle/Mockingbird: Songs of Empowerment* and *You Know What I'm Sayin'?* García Ordaz is a teacher at La Joya Early College High School. He's a songwriter and also a founder of the Rio Grande Valley International Poetry Festival and the Gloria Anzaldúa Legacy Project.

Michelle R. Garza was born and raised in Corpus Christi, TX. Her abuelita instilled a love of birds, and that love for birds is what drew her to the RGV, where she now lives and works as a High School English teacher.

A San Antonio son, **Tomás Julián** seeks to speak to the constant mix of life's joys and woes through the lens of an assimilated Latino millennial seeking to recapture his heritage. He is lover of dogs and butterfingers, Los Spurs and the 2013 & 2016 San Antonio Puro Slam Grand Slam Champion.

ire'ne lara silva is the author of three poetry collections, *furia*, *Blood Sugar Canto*, and *CUICACALLI/House of Song*, an e-chapbook, *Enduring Azucares*, as well as a short story collection, *flesh to bone*, which won the Premio Aztlán. She and poet Dan Vera are also the co-editors of *Imaniman: Poets Writing in the Anzaldúan Borderlands*, a collection of poetry and essays. ire'ne is the recipient of a 2017 NALAC Fund for the Arts Grant, the final recipient of the Alfredo Cisneros del Moral Award, and was the Fiction Finalist for AROHO's 2013 Gift of Freedom Award.

Armando X. Lopez (AXL) has been a practicing attorney in Laredo, Texas for 37 years. His poetry has been published by the Guadalupe Cultural Arts Center in San Antonio as part of its Conjunto Festival. He has been a poet with Laredo Border Slam since 2012 and performed with Laredo Border Slam in Laredo, San Antonio, Houston, Tulsa, and Baton Rouge.

Joaquin Muerte was born in the barrio of San Felipe in Del Rio. He began his professional music career 16 years ago in San Antonio as a street performer playing percussion and guitar. He has been playing music since he was a child and is a founding member of three local bands that compose original music - Los Nahuatlatos, Eddie and the Valiants and the San Antunes. Joaquin is a traditional Danzante conchero, whose roots go back to pre-Hispanic America. He is a community health worker and community organizer in poor communities of color. Joaquin's many other titles include chef, gardener, father, and husband.

Susana Nevarez-Marquez is a first generation Tejana. Inspiration comes from family tales of Durango, Mexico and Robstown, Texas. The aunt who raised her from birth was kidnapped by a Villista soldier during the Mexican Revolution. Taken at only 13 years-old, Maria Nolberta escaped years later when the soldier was killed. Even though she raised Susana from birth, Tia Berta kept her secret until a relative divulged it. Susana never told her aunt that she knew but its knowledge greatly impacted Susana's view of the world. Her poems have been published by VIA's *Poetry on the Move, Love Poems to San Antonio, Voices de la Luna, The Rivard Report, Lone Stars Magazine, Fresh Studies in Rio Grande Valley History* and several chapbooks. Her stories have appeared in the *San Antonio Express-News, Tonantzin, Puro Conjunto* and *Chicken Soup for the Soul*. She frequently participates in open mics around the San Antonio area.

Amalia Ortiz appeared on three seasons of *Russell Simmons Presents Def Poetry* on HBO. She was awarded the 2020 American Book Award for Oral Literature. NBC Latino listed her book, *Rant. Chant. Chisme.* among "10 Great Latino Books of 2015." She won an Alfredo Cisneros Del Moral Grant, a residency at the National Hispanic Cultural Center, the 2015 Writers' League of Texas Poetry Discovery Prize, and the 2018 NALAC Fund for the Arts Grant to film videos for her latest book *The Canción Cannibal Cabaret*. Amalia received her MFA in Creative Writing from The University of Texas Rio Grande Valley.

From Eagle Pass, Texas, **Rita L. Ortiz** is a writer, songwriter, and musician based in San Antonio. Ortiz is currently an English instructor in Palo Alto

College and the lead vocalist for The Velvet Hues, an independent band. Their new album, *Cantares*, was released in April 2020. Ortiz's work includes music, poetry, and film--all which explore identity and language in the context of cultural hybridity, and the surreal and symbolic nature of dreams in connection to epiphany.

Darian Danielle Rodriguez was born and raised in Corpus Christi, TX. her poetry reflects her Chicano upbringing, generational trauma, homophobia, and ultimately love in all its forms. Her hope for her poetry is that little Sadgurlz will find themselves in her corazón and know they are deserving of every sueño the barrio has tried to wake them from.

Odilia Galván Rodríguez, poet, writer, editor, social justice activist, and publisher, is the author of seven volumes of poetry, her latest is, *The Color of Light* FlowerSong Press, 2019. She is co-editor, along with the late Francisco X. Alarcón, of the award-winning *Poetry of Resistance: Voices for Social Justice*, from The University of Arizona Press. Odilia has worked as an editor for various print magazines, most recently as the English edition editor of *Tricontinental Magazine* in Havana, Cuba. She also edits *Cloud Women's Quarterly* and *Anacua Literary Arts Journal* online. Her activist work stems several decades with organizations such as the United Farm Workers of America AFL-CIO. Currently she facilitates creative writing workshops nationally and is the administrator of Poets Responding, on Facebook. Odilia is dedicated to bringing awareness to eco and social justice issues. Her poetry and short fiction are included in many anthologies and literary journals in print and on-line.

Mia Stahl is a queer Latinx graduate of St. Mary's University and a lifelong student of the universe. She has been creatively expressing through poetry since the age of eight but has begun writing spoken word poetry in the last four years. Her passions lie in obtaining the tools needed to support and progress the communities that created her. She is a mosaic of the community that has etched her and she hopes to one day etch the next generation of empowered queer Latinx writers, students and creatives.

Priscilla Celina Suárez was the 2015-17 McAllen Poet Laureate, where she had an opportunity to rediscover the many communities in the Rio Grande Valley. During her childhood, she lived surrounded by the farmlands of the then small colonia of Las Milpas, TX, where she first heard many of the cuentos she shares in her work.

Carmen Tafolla, author of *New & Selected Works* (2018), *This River Here* (2014), *Rebozos* (2012), *The Holy Tortilla & A Pot of Beans: A Feast of Short Fiction* (2008), and 30 other books, Tafolla was 2015 State Poet Laureate of Texas, and the first City Poet Laureate of San Antonio in 2012-2014. A co-founder of CantoMundo, a Latinx poetry space, and recipient of numerous awards, including five International Latino Book Awards and the

Américas Award, she has been recognized by the National Association of Chicana & Chicano Studies for work which "gives voice to the peoples and cultures of this land."

Nicolas Valdez is a San Antonio-based interdisciplinary performance artist. His work focuses on the experience of the communities along the US-Mexico border. An accomplished writer, actor, and accordionist, he is a member of Los Nahuatlatos who have released two full-length albums. His latest production, *Conjunto Blues*, is solo theatrical performance that explores the historical and social conditions that led to the development of Conjunto music as an expression of cultural resistance and liberation.

Eddie Vega is a poet, spoken word artist, storyteller, and educator. His poetry has been displayed on VIA Buses and downtown San Antonio buildings. His first full-length collection of poetry, *Chicharra Chorus*, was published in 2019 by FlowerSong Press and he is the 2021 recipient of the Literary Arts Grant from the Luminaria Artist Foundation. Vega writes about food, Tejano culture, social justice, and the intersections thereof. Known as the Taco-Poet of Texas, he can be found at an open-mic, slam, or taqueria on any given, non-quarantine evening anywhere throughout South Texas. Follow him on social media: @eltacolico

Denisse Zecca is a 25-year-old mother and student born and raised in Edinburg, TX. She is currently attending UTRGV and majoring in English with a concentration in Creative Writing.

www.ingramcontent.com/pod-product-compliance
Lightning Source LLC
Chambersburg PA
CBHW011224120626
46545CB00010B/3142